SIGHTSEERS
ESSENTIAL TRAVEL GUIDES TO THE PAST

PARIS
1789

A GUIDE TO PARIS ON THE EVE OF THE REVOLUTION

RACHEL WRIGHT

KING*f*ISHER

NEW YORK

Editor   Julie Ferris
Senior Designer   Jane Tassie

Consultant   Dylan Rees
Illustrations   Inklink Firenze
Kevin Maddison

KINGFISHER
Larousse Kingfisher Chambers Inc.
95 Madison Avenue
New York, New York 10016

First published in 1999
2 4 6 8 10 9 7 5 3 1
1TR/1298/WKT/UNV(UNV)/140MA

LIBRARY OF CONGRESS CATALOGING-IN-PUBLICATION DATA
Wright, Rachel.
Sightseers : Paris, 1789/Rachel Wright.
p.   cm.
Includes index.
Summary: Uses a travel guide format to show what life was like in
Paris at the time of the French Revolution.
1. Paris (France)—History—1789–1799—Juvenile literature.
2. France—History—Revolution, 1789–1799—Juvenile literature.
3. Paris (France)—Social life and customs—18th century—Juvenile
literature. [1. Paris (France)—Social life and customs—18th
century. 2. France—History—Revolution, 1789–1799.] I. Title.
DC194.W75   1999
944' 36104—dc21 98-39804 CIP AC

ISBN 0-7534-5183-2

Printed in Hong Kong

Contents

Introducing Paris 1789

Paris is both an exciting and dangerous place to visit. The capital of France is one of the most heavily populated cities in Europe and has been the focal point of revolutionary activity this year. Although King Louis XVI has not been overthrown by the revolutionaries, his powers are gradually being removed, as are the privileges of the nobility and the wealthy Roman Catholic Church.

Louis XVI, seen here with his unpopular wife Marie-Antoinette, lost control of Paris because of an unfair tax system.

Keep an eye out for topical cartoons about peasants being oppressed by nobles and bishops. They have been popular all year.

Change your cash into livres, sous, and deniers—the French currency.

Roman Catholicism is France's main religion. The Church owns a lot of land.

Parts of Paris have changed little in the 400 years since the Middle Ages.

If you were hoping to experience life among the French nobility during your visit, you may be disappointed. The recent uprisings against royal rule by ordinary French people have sent a wave of panic through aristocratic circles, and some noble families have already fled the country.

Sightseers' tip

The best way to see Paris is by hot air balloon. This novel form of transportation was invented only six years ago by the Montgolfier brothers and is not widely available. So, make sure you try it if you get the chance.

Travel alert

Visiting a city in the grip of revolution can be dangerous, so be on your guard. After all, it was only a few months ago, in July, that a mob of ordinary Parisians stormed a hated royal fortress called the Bastille to seize gunpowder, and peasants in the country attacked the homes of the rich and powerful.

Medals in the shape of the Bastille, and plates and prints with revolutionary scenes make great souvenirs. For something more unusual, how about a paperweight made from the ruined fortress's stones?

Be prepared for pushing, shoving, and fighting in the long breadlines.

On July 14, the Bastille fortress was captured by a mob of about 900 people.

Read a newspaper to keep up to date with news of the revolution.

Sightseers' tip Make sure you know what the church bells of Paris sound like when they ring the *tocsin*, or alarm. This signal warns Parisians to take up arms.

Don't panic if you see men dressed in uniforms like this. They are members of the National Guard, a peacekeeping force organized by the new revolutionary government. Their job is to prevent popular protests from getting out of hand, and to prevent the king's troops from overthrowing the revolution.

A major problem you will face if your budget is small is the shortage of cheap, tasty bread. Due to recent bad harvests and drought (which left millers unable to grind grain for flour), bread has been overpriced and in short supply for a long time. As it is the main food of most Parisians, this situation has caused riots in the capital and long lines at bakeries. Make sure you get up early to join one of the long breadlines, otherwise you could go hungry.

Getting around Paris

Unlike the outskirts of Paris, the center is crowded, with narrow, dirty streets. Open gutters filled with kitchen water and other waste run along the middle of many streets, so be prepared for unpleasant smells. If you go for a morning stroll, listen for the cry, "Watch out underneath!" It means someone is about to empty a chamber pot out of a window above your head.

Use a sedan chair (a covered chair carried by two men) to travel around crowded streets.

The recent introduction of streetlights means that the narrow streets of Paris are well lit.

Stand clear of fast one-horse carriages, which can splatter you with mud.

The Seine River flows through Paris and gives the city a vital waterway on which to travel, as well as water to drink. The bridges that cross the Seine are often busy.

Traveling from Paris to other cities in France is easiest by stagecoach. Stagecoaches set off from the rue Notre Dames des Victoires each evening, and can carry up to ten passengers, plus luggage. It takes five days to travel over 280 miles to Lyons, but there are places on the way where you can eat and rest.

A stagecoach is faster than a cart or pony carriage, but also more expensive.

Sightseers' tip Don't ruin your best shoes by wading through stinking street gutters. Hire a gutter leaper to carry you piggyback across them instead.

What to wear

If you want to show support for
the revolution during your visit to
Paris, wear the national colors—
red, blue, and white. Known as the
tricolor, these colors have become the
symbol of those in favor of a fairer
system of government.

An elegant outfit made
from tricolor-striped satin
will certainly let everyone
know which side you are
on. You will need to have
it specially made,
however, so it
will set you
back a livre
or two!

Don't worry if you're not sure
whether you want to support the
revolutionaries or the royalists.
Black seems to be a color
worn by both sides.

Avoid cotton clothes in winter—sparks from fires can set them alight.

Check fashion magazines for news of the latest styles.

Dress well—the French spend 15 percent of their wages on clothes.

Sightseers' tip If you want to show support for the king, queen, and aristocracy while visiting Paris, wear a white satin rosette on your hat.

Male visitors should be careful not to wear the wrong type of pants. Only workers in manual trades wear long pants. The aristocracy and wealthier workers wear culottes, or knee-breeches.

The red and blue of the tricolor are the colors of Paris, and the white is the color of the king. Many men are wearing a tricolor rosette on their hats to show their commitment to the revolution. A few have gone one step further, wearing shoe buckles shaped like the towers of the Bastille. Female travelers who want to make a similar fashion statement could wear one of the new hats shaped like a Bastille tower and trimmed with a tricolor ribbon.

Poor people, such as peasants, have neither the time nor the money to spend on fashionable clothes, so they choose more practical styles.

Why not buy a fan with a pro-revolution or pro-royalty design on it as a souvenir?

11

Food, drink, and shopping

Street traders are a common sight in Paris.

If your budget is too tight to afford meat, let alone a restaurant meal, you'll have to survive mainly on thin soup and bread. To improve your lot, try to get invited to dinner at a wealthy home. That way you'll be able to enjoy more refined dishes such as roast meats, oysters, and desserts.

Sightseers' tip

If you buy fresh meat that you don't plan to eat right away, cover it with salt to preserve it. If the meat is left for very long, you may need to use expensive spices to disguise the taste.

Paris is famous for beautiful and expensive porcelain, which is made in the factory at Sèvres, just outside the city.

Buying high-quality goods should not be a problem as there are many skilled craftsmen and workshops in Paris. Luxury goods such as tapestries, wigs, and silk are readily available. Traders need your custom—recent events have not helped business.

Parisians love wine, and drink about 700,000 liters of it a year.

Many workers spend half their pay buying bread for their families.

Avoid Les Halles if you can't face seeing cattle being butchered on the street.

Les Halles is *the* place to shop if you are cooking for yourself. The capital's main marketplace, it is made up of 20 small, noisy markets. Goods from outside Paris reach Les Halles via the Seine River.

Alongside the professional tradesmen, there are people selling cheap, homegrown produce in Les Halles. Fresh meat and wine are also available in the bustling markets.

13

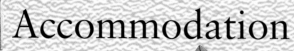

Accommodation

There are all kinds of rooms to rent in Paris, so you should be able to find something affordable. The best rooms are on the lower floors of a house and are occupied by lawyers, bankers, and the like, while the cheaper rooms at the top are rented by poorer workers.

If you stay in poorer lodgings, you may not be very comfortable. Many poor families live in just one or two rooms. They have little furniture, bare walls, and their beds often have no covers.

If you are lucky enough to be asked to stay in an aristocrat's home, you will see just how well the very rich live. Their elegant sitting rooms are filled with delicate pieces of furniture, paintings, porcelain, and large, expensive mirrors.

Traffic doesn't stop at night, so avoid lodgings with streets on all sides.

Don't forget, you will have to buy candles and oil lamps for light.

If you have no money, go to a poorhouse for charitable help.

The wealthy, like the poor, rely on open fires to keep them warm in winter. Unlike the poor however, the rich have servants to light their fires for them.

Sightseers' tip

Check to see whether the cellar of the place where you are staying is used as a cesspool. If it is, empty your chamber pot into it. Cesspools are emptied at night by special cleaners.

One of the delights of staying with the rich is that you get to use their bathtub. Very few people can afford to pay for buckets of water to be delivered to their homes. If you don't have access to a private bath, you can use one of the city's indoor public baths. There are also public baths on the Seine River, where you can rent a cabin built on a barge into which river water is pumped.

A chair in the new French colors or a fashionable, oval-shaped sofa make great, if expensive, souvenirs.

The Palais-Royal

The Duke of Orléans, owner of the Palais-Royal and relative of the king, turned the palace gardens into a popular fair to help himself out of a financial fix.

No trip to Paris is complete without a visit to the Palais-Royal in the center of the city. There you'll find cafés, restaurants, theaters, gambling dens, museums, private clubs, and shops galore, selling everything from candy and glasses to bear grease to stop your hair from falling out.

You should be able to find luxurious lodgings near the Palais-Royal, but they are not cheap.

See short plays about French history at the Children's Museum in the Palais-Royal.

Keep an eye out for dishonest storekeepers, who may try to pass off copper as gold.

Sightseers' tip Don't miss the little cannon at the Palais-Royal which fires each day at noon when it is struck by the rays of the sun.

The Palais-Royal is *the* place to go to catch up on the latest news, gossip, and rumors. Political pamphlets and newspapers are easy to find there, and passionate speakers have been known to draw large crowds by giving speeches in one of the many cafés at the palace. The lively political debates can often get very heated, so don't be startled if cups and saucers are thrown.

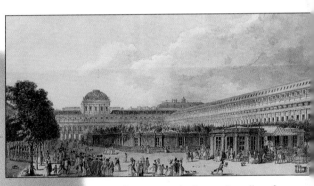

You'll see people from all walks of life in the Palais-Royal's extensive arcades and gardens.

Be sure to treat yourself to a cup of delicious chocolate served from an elegant pot.

The boulevards

L ike the Palais-Royal, the boulevards are well worth a visit. Everyone, from well-dressed ladies to ragged street children, flocks to these animated avenues, which are crammed with busy cafés, popular theaters, and exciting street entertainment.

Look out for girls with magic lanterns on their backs. They play hand organs to let you know they're coming. For six deniers, you can peer into their candlelit boxes and see painted slides of faraway places.

The boulevards are crowded with traders and peddlers. If you get thirsty, keep your eyes open for a drink peddler. You'll recognize him by the goblets chained to his belt, which he fills up from his portable kettle. If you're feeling lucky, keep your ears open for men announcing lottery winners in the street.

Many people go to the boulevards simply to stroll around, look at each another, and enjoy the buzz of the crowd. However, there is also plenty of entertainment on offer. You'll find everything from waxworks, animal fights, and exhibitions of unusual people, to amazing illusion shows, including one where glass and mirrors are used to create the effect of fireworks.

Listen for the sound of the hurdy-gurdy being played on the boulevards.

If you fancy a day at the horse races, head for nearby Vincennes.

Hold on to your purse. Pickpockets often work in crowded streets.

A visit to one of the city's very fashionable public gardens makes a refreshing break from exploring the Parisian streets. The Tuileries Gardens, which are open to well-to-do workers on Sundays, are often used for hot air balloon takeoffs.

Sightseers' tip

Avoid the boulevards if you have a headache. The sound of people shouting at the entertainers, musicians playing for the café crowds, and traders yelling about their wares will only make it worse.

The theater

François-Joseph Talma is *the* actor to see. His natural acting style is seen as less pompous than that of other actors.

A visit to Paris would not be complete without a trip to the theater. There are three major theaters in the city, and a number of smaller ones. Two of the major theaters, the Opéra and the Comédie Italienne, specialize in ballet and opera, while the Comédie Française is famous for staging well-written plays.

Why not go to a piano recital? Perfected in 1709, the piano now rivals the harpsichord in popularity.

At present, the three major theaters still have the sole right to stage certain types of shows. For example, the Comédie Française is the only theater allowed to stage the great French tragedies and comedies, although this hasn't stopped other theaters from performing them. The smaller boulevard theaters are best known for their lively and irreverent plays, often poking fun at officials and professional people. These shows often have a revolutionary theme now.

Look for plays by Molière—one of France's best comic playwrights.

Be warned—theater audiences will hiss and jeer at shows they don't like.

The royal family has a theater of their own at the Palace at Versailles.

Sightseers' tip

Look in newspapers, such as the *Journal de Paris*, to find out what's on at the theater. Don't forget that the Comédie Française has recently been renamed Théâtre de la Nation.

Expect mixed audiences—both rich and poor go to the theater. The best seats at the plush Comédie Française are in the balconies at the sides. The less well-off stand in the rowdy *parterre* (pit) in front of the stage.

Notre Dame

Dominating the Paris skyline, the Catholic cathedral of Notre Dame is by far the most famous church in France. It is an astounding sight, and undoubtedly an essential part of any visit to the city. Famed for its Gothic architecture, construction began in 1163 and took nearly two hundred years to complete.

Notre Dame is renowned for its stunning 13th-century stained glass rose windows, which flood the cathedral with multicolored light.

With its high, vaulted ceilings, Notre Dame is a breathtaking example of Gothic architecture.

Inside Notre Dame you will find tombs and statues of kings and nobles. Before the revolution, people believed that the king's right to rule was given by God, and not by the will of his subjects.

Choose a bright day to see the stained glass windows in all their glory.

Inside Notre Dame you'll find beautiful religious paintings and statues.

You can watch the royal family attend church at their palace at Versailles.

Pay special attention to the royal statues and tombs in the cathedral as they may not survive the revolutionary fervor. The new government has declared that all men are born equal and that special privileges will be abolished. It has also attacked the wealth and power of the Church.

The winglike supports that jut out from the outside walls are called flying buttresses. They are a common feature of Gothic churches.

The spectacular Church of Sainte-Geneviève is due for completion next year. It has been built in the memory of Geneviève, the patron saint of Paris.

The government has already abolished taxes paid to the powerful Church and looks set to sell the Church's lands to raise money. It is probable that the treasures in Notre Dame will not be there much longer.

Sightseers' tip

If you get lost in the city, look for Notre Dame's needle spire. It can be seen from all over Paris and may help you get your bearings.

The Louvre

The royal art collection on show at the Louvre Palace in the heart of Paris is a sight not to be missed. The first king to collect art for the Louvre was Charles V in the 1300s. Since then, other royals have added to the collection with impressive works of art by the great artists of their day.

Sightseers' tip If you want to talk intelligently about modern art, remember that portraits and paintings of landscapes are becoming more and more popular. The increase in portraits is because the rich middle class wants to be remembered as the new upper class.

It is well worth attending a salon, if invited. They are regular meetings, held in a wealthy person's home, to talk about art or politics.

Of all the artists with a studio at the Louvre, Jacques-Louis David is the most famous. His painting nicknamed "Brutus" caused great excitement when it was exhibited this summer. It is about an Ancient Roman named Brutus who executed his sons because they were plotting to restore the monarchy in Rome.

Look out for Leonardo da Vinci's famous portrait *Mona Lisa*, in the Louvre.

If you're feeling hungry, Les Halles is only a stone's throw away from the palace.

Jacques-Louis David's painting "Brutus" is over nine feet high.

As you stroll through the great gallery of the Louvre, take time to admire the glass panels built into the ceiling. This lighting system has only recently been installed as part of the palace refurbishments.

David's powerful painting "Brutus" captures the moment when Brutus' dead sons are carried home on stretchers.

The Palace of Versailles

About two hours from the center of Paris, the Palace of Versailles is easy to reach by coach and horses and makes an ideal day trip. Home to King Louis XVI, Queen Marie-Antoinette, and the French court, Versailles is generally regarded as the most spectacular royal palace in Europe.

Many rooms in the palace have beautiful, painted ceilings.

Until recent events, the royal court was the center of power in France.

Illuminations (light shows) are often held in the ornate gardens.

The palace is full of priceless paintings and sculpture.

Originally a modest medieval château, Versailles now boasts 2,143 windows, 1,252 fireplaces, 67 staircases, extensive gardens, and lavishly decorated state rooms.

Sightseers' tip
To tour the palace and grounds of Versailles, you must be decently dressed, and no beggars are allowed.

Created by Marie-Antoinette, the fairy-tale village in the palace grounds has a working farm, a mill, and very well-dressed peasants.

If you have influential friends at court, ask them if you might be given the honor of attending the king's *lever* (morning rising), or his *coucher* (going to bed). These ceremonies are the most important in the court's day.

A spectacular venue for elegant balls, the 220-foot long Hall of Mirrors links the king's apartments to those of the queen.

Survival guide

If you can't live without all the comforts and conveniences of home, then revolutionary France may not be the ideal vacation place for you. Make sure you are prepared for frustrations and discomforts before you leave.

Administration

The revolution is bringing about radical changes in the way that France is governed. As the king's power ebbs away, ordinary people are gaining more influence over how their country is run.

Getting to grips with the 60,000 or so different measures of weight in France is hard, but don't worry—a committee is trying to introduce a simpler system of weights and measures.

Law and order

There are gruesome punishments for dangerous criminals in France. They may be burned with hot irons, or sentenced to death by hanging.

Nobles who are found guilty of murder are beheaded with a sword instead of being hanged. However, a Parisian doctor named Joseph Guillotine is trying to introduce a beheading machine with a slicing blade, so that all condemned may enjoy a quick and painless execution.

Health

The healthcare system in France is very poorly funded, so it is a good idea to make sure that you are in good shape before you go. French doctors believe that having too much bad blood is the cause of many illnesses. They'll probably cut open your veins or put bloodsucking leeches on your skin if you get sick.

Don't complain about a toothache! There are no anesthetics, so dentists pull out aching teeth without the use of painkillers.

29

? Souvenir quiz

Now that your trip to Paris is over, your suitcase is probably full of souvenirs. Give this special souvenir quiz a try to see how much you can remember from your visit.

1. In 1789, the poor of Paris spent most of their money on food. Which food formed the basis of their diet?

a) Bitter chocolate, which was boiled with water to make a drink.

b) Bread, which was often hard to find—and even harder to digest.

c) Broiled beef and wine, which were bought from Les Halles in the heart of Paris.

2. Which form of public transportation did Parisians use when they wanted to travel out of the city to one of France's main cities quickly?

a) A stagecoach pulled by a team of horses.

b) A hot air balloon which took off from one of the city's public gardens.

c) A sedan chair carried by a team of human runners.

3. For what reason did people flock to the arcades and gardens of the Palais-Royal?

a) To hear political gossip and read political pamphlets printed by underground presses.

b) To eat and drink and see the other people who gathered there.

c) To see theater performances and to enjoy a bit of gambling.

4. Which group of Frenchmen wore long pants instead of culottes, or knee breeches?

a) Workers in manual trades, such as laborers and craftsmen.

b) Wealthy, middle class workers such as lawyers, bankers, merchants, and factory owners.

c) Members of the royal court and other nobles.

5. Which of these churches was still being built in 1789?

a) The basilica of Saint-Denis, which was occupied by royal troops early in the revolution.

b) The great cathedral of Notre Dame.

c) The church of Sainte-Geneviève, which was turned into a burial place for great Frenchmen during the revolution, and renamed the Panthéon.

6. Which of these events did not happen in the summer of 1789?

a) The ransacking of rich country homes by French peasants.

b) The capture of the Bastille by a mob of about 900 people.

c) The execution of King Louis XVI.

7. Jacques-Louis David's painting "Brutus" caused great excitement this summer. What is it about?

a) A revolutionary named Brutus who stormed the Bastille.

b) An Ancient Roman named Brutus who had his sons killed.

c) An aristocrat named Brutus being beheaded with a sword.

8. If you wanted to see a play by Molière or a performance by François-Joseph Talma, where could you look for theater information?

a) *Pariscope.*

b) *Le Figaro.*

c) *Journal de Paris.*

9. During the revolution red, white, and blue became the national colors of France. What did these color represent?

a) Blue was the color of the royal family, and red and white the colors of Paris.

b) Red and blue were the colors of Paris, and white was the color of the king.

c) White was the color of Paris, and red and blue the colors of the French country.

Index

Acknowledgments

Inklink Firenze illustrators
Simone Boni, Alessandro Rabatti, Lorenzo Pieri, Luigi
Critone, Lucia Mattioli, Francisco Petracchi, Theo
Caneschi.

The consultant
Dylan Rees BA, MEd, PGCE is Principal Examiner,
French Revolution, WJEC.

Picture credits
b = bottom, c = center, l = left, r = right, t = top
p.4tc E.T. Archive/Musée Carnavalet, Paris; p.4tr E.T.
Archive/V & A; p.6tl Photothèque des Musées de la
Ville de Paris, Pierrain; p.6c Bulloz; p.9tr Jean-Loup
Charmet/ Musée Carnavalet, Paris; p.11tl & tc,
Museum fuer Deutsche Geschichte, Berlin/AKG;
p. 11bl Bulloz; p.12c Porzellansammlung, Dresden/
AKG; p.12tl E.T. Archive/Musée Carnavalet, Paris;
p.16tl Musée Conde, Chantilly/AKG/Erich Lessing;
p.17cr Jean-Loup Charmet/Musée Carnavalet, Paris;
p.20tl Bibliotheque de l'Arsenal/AKG; p.20c
Historisches Museum der Stadt, Vienna/The
Bridgeman Art Library, London; p.22tr & cl Bulloz;
p.25tr Louvre, Paris/ AKG/Erich Lessing; p. 26
RMN/Mercator; p.27 RMN.

*Every effort has been made to trace the copyright
holders of the photographs. The publishers apologize
for any inconvenience caused.*

Souvenir quiz answers

1 = b) 2 = a) 3 = a, b & c) 4 = a) 5 = c) 6 = c) 7 = b) 8 = c) 9 = b)

*The setting for this
Sightseers guide is
September 1789.*